VENUS

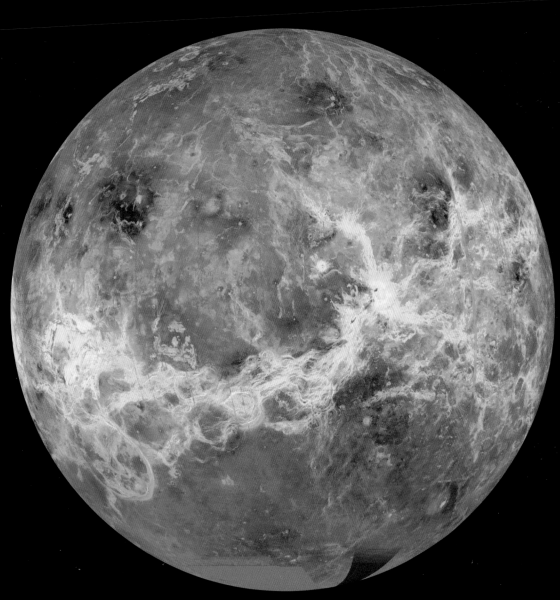

Published by Heinemann Library,
a division of Reed Educational & Professional Publishing,
Halley Court, Jordan Hill,
Oxford OX2 8EJ, UK
Visit our website at www.heinemann.co.uk/library

Produced by Brown Partworks
Project Editor: Ben Morgan
Deputy Editor: Sally McFall
Managing Editor: Anne O'Daly
Designer: Steve Wilson
Illustrator: Mark Walker
Picture Researcher: Helen Simm
Consultant: Peter Bond

© 2001 Brown Partworks Limited

Printed in Singapore

ISBN 0 431 12261 X (hardback)
06 05 04 03 02 01
10 9 8 7 6 5 4 3 2 1

ISBN 0 431 122709 (paperback)
06 05 04 03 02 01
10 9 8 7 6 5 4 3 2 1

British Library Cataloguing in Publication Data

Sparrow, Giles
   Venus. – (Exploring the solar system)
   1. Venus (Planet) – Juvenile literature
   I. Title
   523.4'2

BELOW: *The planets of the Solar System, shown in order from the Sun:
Mercury, Venus, Earth, Mars, Jupiter, Saturn, Uranus, Neptune, Pluto.*

CONTENTS

*Some words are shown in bold, **like this**.*
You can find out what they mean by looking in the glossary.

Venus is the brightest object in the night sky, after the Moon. It can be bright enough to cast shadows on Earth, and you can sometimes see it during the day if you know where to look. Venus is the second planet from the Sun and Earth is the third. Because Venus is closer to the Sun than Earth, it always appears near the Sun in the sky. The best times to see Venus are just after sunset or just before sunrise.

In some ways Venus is like Earth's twin. It is the closest planet to us and is only slightly smaller than Earth. Venus and Earth are both made of rock, and both planets have a thick, cloudy **atmosphere**.

Like all the planets in the Solar System, Venus travels around the Sun along a path called an **orbit**, and the time it takes to make one orbit is the length of its year. While Earth orbits the Sun in 365 days, Venus takes just 225 days.

Venus stays about 108 million kilometres (67 million miles) from the Sun throughout its orbit, but its distance from Earth is always changing.

Getting to Venus

The time it takes to reach Venus depends on your method of transport, and on the positions of Venus and Earth in their orbits when you set off.

Distance from Earth to Venus
Closest   **42 million km (26 million miles)**
Furthest   **257 million km (160 million miles)**

By car at 113 km per hour (70 miles per hour)
Closest   **42 years**
Furthest   **260 years**

By rocket at 11 km per second (7 miles per second)
Closest   **43 days**
Furthest   **265 days**

Time for radio signals to reach Venus (at the speed of light)
Closest   **2 min. 20 sec.**
Furthest   **14 min. 20 sec.**

Distance from the Sun

The diagram shows how far the planets are from the Sun. Venus is one of the inner planets, like our Earth. It may look close to us on this scale, but it is many millions of kilometres away.

Sun   Mercury   Venus   Earth   Mars   Jupiter   Saturn

0   1000 (621)   2000 (1243)
Distance in millions of kilometres (millions of miles)

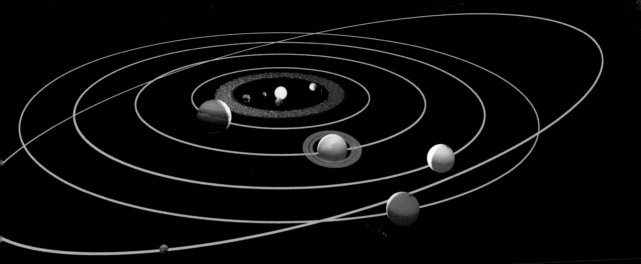

When Venus and Earth line up on the same side of the Sun they are about 41 million kilometres (26 million miles) apart, a distance that would take just over two years to travel at the speed of Concorde (2179 kilometres per hour, or 1354 miles per hour). But when Venus and Earth are on opposite sides of the Sun they are 258 million kilometres (160 million miles) apart, or a thirteen-year journey at the speed of Concorde.

Imagine you're about to join a **mission** to Venus. You'll have to time the departure date for when Venus is closest to Earth, but the trip will still take months. Although your rocket can travel at 11 kilometres per second, you'll be flying in a spiral path towards Venus, not a straight line. You will also need a powerful rocket: Venus moves faster through space than Earth, so your ship will have to catch up with it. In space there is no **gravity**, so everything is weightless and floats in midair. Zero gravity can cause your bones and muscles to weaken from lack of exercise, so your ship will spin around to create **artificial gravity**.

*The Solar System is made up of the Sun, nine planets and the asteroid belt – a ring of **debris** that travels in a circle between Mars and Jupiter. All the planets go around the Sun in giant circles called orbits.*

Size compared to Earth

Venus' diameter:
12,103 km
(7520 miles)

Earth's diameter:
12,756 km
(7926 miles)

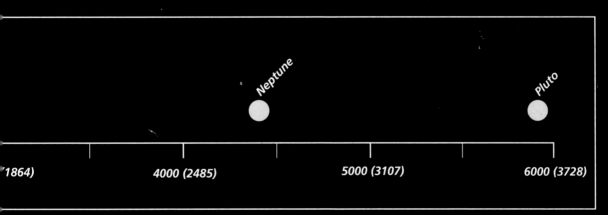

Neptune

Pluto

1864)   4000 (2485)   5000 (3107)   6000 (3728)

First view

As your ship leaves Earth's **orbit**, Venus shines brilliantly above the horizon. You're leaving when Venus and Earth are close, so Venus is at its brightest. When Venus is on the far side of the Sun it is noticeably dimmer but still one of the brightest objects in the sky.

As well as changing in brightness, Venus seems to change shape. Like the Moon, it has **phases** – it transforms from a **crescent** through a semicircle to a full circle, and back again, each time it goes around the Sun. The phases happen because our view from Earth shows different amounts of Venus' daylit half. When Venus is on directly the opposite side of the Sun, the daylit side faces us, but we cannot see it because it is hidden by the Sun's glare. When both planets are on the same side of the Sun, most of Venus' day side faces away from us, but the planet is so much closer that it is still bigger and brighter in the sky.

As the long journey drags on, Venus gets a little brighter every day. Before long you can see the planet's phases without binoculars, but you can't yet make out details on the brilliant sunlit side.

*Powerful rockets are vital to launch your ship on the **mission** to Venus. After escaping Earth's **gravity**, the rockets burn gently to cruise through space.*

ABOVE: *The Moon and Venus (top) are the brightest objects in Earth's night sky. Venus usually appears around sunset or sunrise, when it is often mistaken for a star.*

Getting closer

Soon Venus has grown to a brilliant circle, the size of the Moon in Earth's sky. Venus reflects eleven times as much sunlight as the Moon, making it painfully bright to look at.

Using coloured filters to block out most of the light, you see the first signs of detail on the planet. But the surface detail keeps changing. You soon realize why: Venus is completely covered by clouds. No matter where you look, there are no gaps where you can see the surface below.

The most obvious patterns on Venus are trails of darker clouds that curve towards the **poles**, producing a distinctive V-shape. You can see the V-shape most clearly by using a special camera that detects **ultraviolet light**, a type of light that is normally invisible to the human eye. Venus' cloud patterns change quickly as furious winds blow the cloud tops around the planet. By watching closely you calculate how fast these high winds are. At 360 kilometres per hour (225 miles per hour), they reach faster speeds than wind in a hurricane on Earth.

Looking away from the daylit half of Venus, you discover to your surprise that the planet's night side isn't completely black – it shines with a pale glow. Astronomers have known about this strange effect, called the **ashen light**, for hundreds of years, but they have yet to find out what causes it. It remains one of the oldest unsolved mysteries in the Solar System.

Venus' surface is completely hidden by clouds. Raging winds sweep the highest clouds into dark streaks that curve towards the poles.

Through the clouds

ABOVE: *Venus is a world of volcanoes. Perhaps there are 'waterfalls' of lava on Venus, like this one on Hawaii.*

Finally your spaceship goes into **orbit** around Venus. With the rocket engines turned off, you find yourself weightless again. Smoggy clouds completely hide Venus' surface, so you have no idea what might lurk beneath. Before risking a descent into the unknown, you decide to send a **space probe**.

The probe's temperature shoots up as it ploughs into the upper **atmosphere**. The intense heat suggests that Venusian air must be much more **dense** than Earth's. Chemical sensors indicate that the choking air is 96 per cent **carbon dioxide**.

After the probe has entered the atmosphere, the heat begins to fade. The probe releases a parachute to slow its fall and its camera switches on. Suddenly you see thick yellow clouds rushing upwards on your monitor. Unlike Earth's clouds of water, these are made of **sulphuric acid**.

Several minutes later the probe breaks out of the clouds and into clear air. Now you can see all the way to the ground, but the picture is blurred by a shimmering heat haze. As the probe falls further, the strange Venusian landscape gradually begins to clear.

Under the murky yellow sky, a desert of brown rock stretches in all directions. Blues and greens – the colours of water and life – are completely missing. But the ground is far from flat. There are rolling hills, mountain ranges and the unmistakable cone shapes of volcanoes. Directly below is a huge volcano belching smoke into the air. The crater in its peak is brimming with glowing orange **lava**, and waterfalls of lava are cascading down its side.

Suddenly lightning is flashing everywhere and the probe's camera begins to shake wildly. Its microphones pick up the fierce crash of thunder – yet there are no storm clouds. Soon the probe drops out of this mysterious zone of lightning with no storms.

At last, the probe hits the ground with a jolt. The temperature reached a searing 475°C (890°F) during the fall – much hotter than an oven – but now it's too high for the probe to measure. Venus' surface is not just hot enough to fry an egg, it's hot enough to melt your probe! Seconds later, the picture on the monitor disappears.

*About 85 per cent of Venus'
surface is covered with solidified
lava from volcanoes, like this lava
flow on a volcano on Hawaii. As
lava cools it turns into a type of
rock called igneous rock.*

As your **space probe** discovered, the surface of Venus is
extremely dangerous. In fact, Venus is the most deadly
planet in the Solar System. If you took a walk on the
planet you would die instantly. The immense air pressure
would crush your body, the scorching heat would burn
you to a crisp and the acid in Venusian air would dissolve
your lungs and skin. Even the
best possible spacesuits would
be unable to keep you alive
for more than a few seconds.

However, we can take an
imaginary tour of Venus if we
suppose that your suit and
craft are made of a newly
discovered material that
withstands incredible heat and
pressure. So, following in the
probe's path, you make a
careful descent through the
clouds. You decide to fly past
some of the volcanoes before
landing. As on Earth, the
tallest volcanoes are **shield volcanoes** – huge cones
of solidified **lava** with circular craters at the top.
The lava from these mountainous volcanoes has
flowed out across wide plains that
stretch for many kilometres.

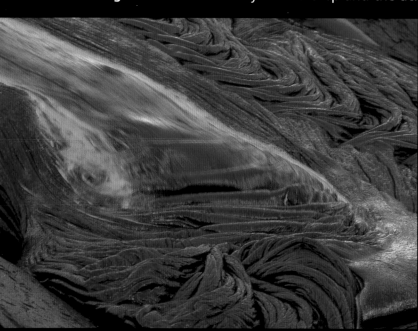

BELOW: *Venus' tallest volcano,
Maat Mons, towers over the
landscape in this 3-D view from
the* Magellan *space probe.*

You see other volcanoes that look very different, like vast, sunken rings with cracks around their edges. These flat volcanoes can measure hundreds of kilometres across.

Venus is also dotted with small volcanoes, many of which are in clusters. Some are miniature shield volcanoes surrounded by plains of solidified lava. Others are dome-shaped. Called pancake domes, these formed from thick, syrupy lava that did not flow very far before it hardened. The air above the active volcanoes is full of lightning. The collision between ash particles rising in the hot air causes a build-up of static charge, which is released in the form of lightning bolts.

Finally you land the ship in a flat area. Venus' **gravity** is similar to Earth's, but you feel heavy when you put on your bulky spacesuit. It gets worse when you step outside – walking through the thick Venusian air is like wading through soup. The ground is treacherous, covered with slabs of rock that you must walk on like stepping stones, taking care not to trip up.

ABOVE: *Venus' 'pancake domes' are small volcanoes that formed from sticky lava. The top picture is a computer-generated 3-D view. The bottom picture is an aerial view from a space probe.*

Awake or asleep?

*Astronomers do not know for sure if any of Venus' volcanoes are still active today, but it does seem likely. Space probes falling through the atmosphere have encountered fierce lightning above volcanoes, which scientists think could be caused by an updraft of hot dust and ash from eruptions. Scientists have also recently recorded a sudden rise of sulphur in Venus' **atmosphere**, and volcanoes are the most likely suspects for its source. To top it off, Venus has over 1600 major volcanic features. With so many volcanoes, could they all really be lying **dormant**?*

Plains and Craters

The landscape around you is a barren desert, bare rock and dust stretching as far as you can see. The light level is similar to an overcast day on Earth, but Venus' yellow clouds cast a sickly hue over the lifeless world.

Although Venus has thousands of volcanoes, most of the planet's surface is made up of flat plains like the site you've landed on. The broken rocks at your feet are the remains of a vast **lava** flood that covered the plain millions of years ago. As the lava cooled and solidified, it shrank and cracked into flat plates of rock.

Walking is too much effort, so you return to your ship and climb aboard a special four-wheeled buggy that you can drive like a car. The thick, heat-resistant tires have no difficulty coping with the rocky terrain. You decide to drive toward a high ridge at the end of the plain.

Three huge impact craters are visible in this view across a Venusian plain. The bottom crater is 37 kilometres (23 miles) wide.

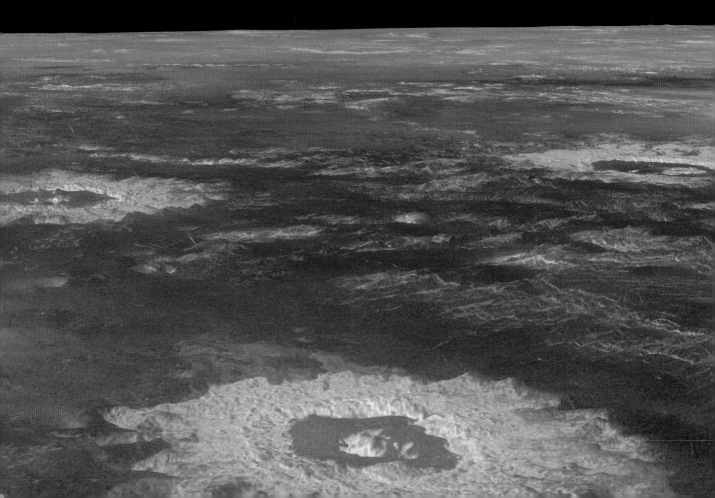

One thing you'd noticed during your flight was the lack of **impact craters** on Venus. Impact craters are the pits made by rocks from space, or **meteorites**, that hit the ground. But when you reach the top of the ridge you realize you've discovered an enormous one. The ridge is the rim of a crater about 5 kilometres (3 miles) wide. This is as small as impact craters get on Venus – only large meteorites pass through the thick **atmosphere** without burning up, so all the craters are huge.

You decide to take a drive around the crater rim, enjoying the sweeping views on both sides. Halfway around, you make an interesting discovery. A vast field of rubble stretches away from the rim and over the plain beyond. This is the material blasted from the ground when the crater formed. The material was flung out to one side only, so perhaps the meteorite hit the ground at an angle.

On your way back to the ship you take a detour to examine a wide crack zig-zagging across the plain. You park next to it and step to the edge to look down, but you jump back in horror at what you see. At the bottom is a river of scalding orange lava that has melted its way through the ground. Before boarding the ship, you scoop up a few rocks and a sample of soil to analyse. These will give you some clues about what Venus is made of.

ABOVE: *Dickinson Crater is 69 kilometres (43 miles) wide. Ejected material lies to the crater's right, suggesting the meteorite hit the ground at an angle.*

Names on Venus
Venus is named for a goddess of love. To match the planet's female name, features on Venus have female names too. For instance, the volcano Maat Mons is named for the Egyptian goddess of truth, and there are craters named for Eve and Cleopatra, as well as a volcanic feature named for the ballerina Anna Pavlova (right). A mountain or volcano is a Mons, a canyon is a Chasma and highlands are called Terrae.

What's inside Venus?

The samples you collected are **igneous** rock, which forms when molten rock, such as **lava**, cools down and solidifies. Your instruments reveal that the samples are a type of igneous rock known as basalt, which is common on Earth. The presence of basalt on Venus suggests that the planet may have a composition similar to that of Earth.

The outer part of Venus is a mostly solid layer of rock called the **crust**, which is about 40 kilometres (25 miles) thick. If you could look inside the crust you would find it peppered with chambers of molten rock called **magma**. These magma chambers feed volcanoes on the surface.

The interior of Venus is probably similar to that of Earth, with a thin crust of rock overlaying a thick mantle and a huge molten core. The inner part of the core may be solid, but no one knows for sure.

Below the crust is the **mantle**, which is about 3000 kilometres (1900 miles) deep. This is an extremely hot region, where semimolten rock churns around like a thick, sticky liquid. The rock in the mantle transports heat towards the surface by **convection**, the process where hot materials rise up and cold ones sink down to take their place. The tops of convection currents, where hot material is closest to the surface, are called hot spots. The hot spots create the magma chambers that feed volcanoes, and they sometimes push the entire crust upward and make the ground bulge.

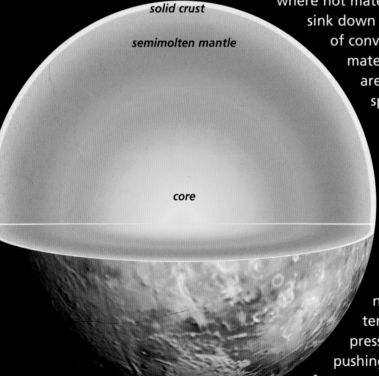

solid crust

semimolten mantle

core

At the centre of Venus is the **core**, an intensely hot ball of molten metal, mostly nickel and iron. The core's temperature is kept high by the pressure of Venus' upper layers pushing down on it. No one knows for sure whether the core is liquid, solid or only partially solidified, like Earth's

Earth's interior is split into separate layers, with heavy substances like metals concentrated in the core and lighter rock in the mantle and crust. The core is only partially solidified, forming an inner and outer core.

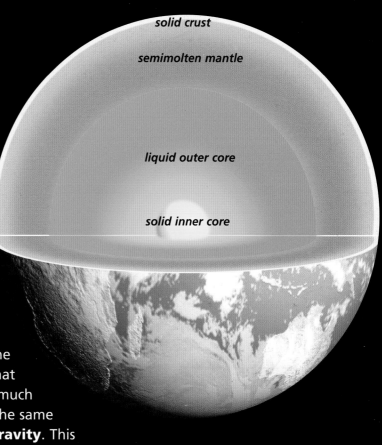

solid crust

semimolten mantle

liquid outer core

solid inner core

Most theories about the internal structure of Venus come from comparison with Earth. There are a number of reasons why astronomers think the interior of the two planets may be alike. Venus and Earth are thought to have formed in a similar way to each other and in the same part of the Solar System, so the materials that make up the planets should be much the same. Also, Venus is about the same size as Earth and has a similar **gravity**. This means that the materials that make up the planets would sift up or down to end up in similar layers within the planets' interiors.

How volcanoes form

Volcanoes form when molten rock from deep underground oozes up through a crack in a planet's surface. The molten rock bursts out of the ground as lava and runs across the surrounding landscape, cooling down and solidifying as it goes. Each time the volcano erupts, more lava builds up. If the lava is very fluid it spreads out rapidly, building up in the middle to form a cone. The end result is a cone-shaped hill or mountain known as a **shield volcano**. *If the lava is sticky and thick, though, it does not make it as far away from the crack, and instead builds up into a rounded dome.*

How Venus formed

Like all the other planets, Venus formed about 4.5 billion years ago in a cloud of gas and dust that was **orbiting** a young star: the Sun. The inner planets of the Solar System – Mercury, Venus, Earth and Mars – formed in a similar way, as small dust particles in the cloud collided together to form clumps that gradually increased in size.

Some of these clumps grew into **planetesimals** – large lumps of rock that had enough **gravity** to pull in material from the cloud around them. Sometimes the planetesimals collided with each other and stuck together. The collisions released heat, so as these miniplanets got larger, they also got hotter. So much heat was released in this way that the young planets turned into molten balls of rock. Under the influence of gravity, heavier **elements** sank to the centre and lighter ones floated on top.

ABOVE: *Planets and stars form in vast gas clouds called nebulas. The Hubble Space Telescope took this picture of a newborn star in the Lagoon Nebula.*

Dating the surface

Astronomers can date a planet's surface by counting its **impact craters**. Big impacts, such as this one in the Great Sandy Desert of western Australia, have occurred at a fairly steady rate for billions of years, so the more craters a planet has, the older its surface must be. Although most **meteors** burn up in Venus' atmosphere, enough big craters have formed for geologists to estimate the surface as about 500 million years old, which is young compared to the planet's age of 4.5 billion years.

The distribution of craters gives more clues to Venus' history. If one part of the planet's surface was slightly older than the others, then we would expect it to have more craters. It turns out that the highlands have slightly more craters than average, indicating that they formed just before the plains. However, most of Venus' craters are scattered completely randomly, suggesting that nearly the whole planet was flooded with lava about 500 million years ago.

Unidentical twins

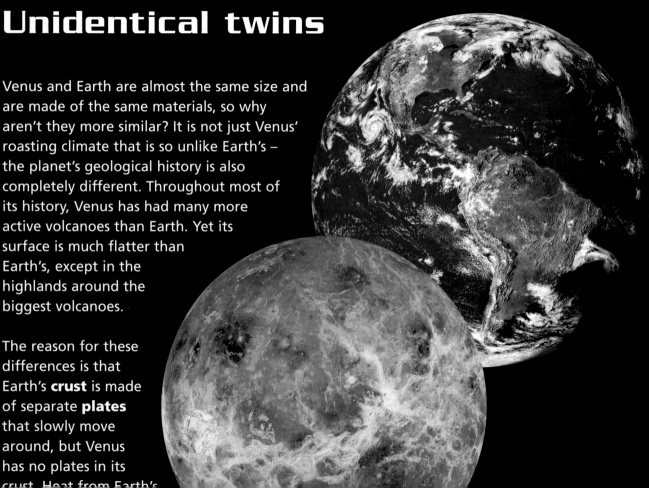

Venus and Earth are almost the same size and are made of the same materials, so why aren't they more similar? It is not just Venus' roasting climate that is so unlike Earth's – the planet's geological history is also completely different. Throughout most of its history, Venus has had many more active volcanoes than Earth. Yet its surface is much flatter than Earth's, except in the highlands around the biggest volcanoes.

The reason for these differences is that Earth's **crust** is made of separate **plates** that slowly move around, but Venus has no plates in its crust. Heat from Earth's

A day on Venus

Venus has one of the strangest daytimes in the Solar System. During your trip on the surface you may have noticed that the Sun, faintly visible through the thick clouds, never moved. Although Venus' upper cloud layers whirl around the planet rapidly, the planet below them stays almost still.

The length of a day on a planet is the time between one sunrise and the next. On most planets this is about the same as the time taken for the planet to make one complete **rotation** – something called the **sidereal day**. However, on Venus the sidereal daylength and the true daylength are very different. This is because Venus rotates very slowly, taking 243 Earth days to make one complete turn. But a Venusian year (the time Venus takes to orbit the Sun once) lasts only 225 Earth days, so Venus' year is shorter than its sidereal day. The combination of short year and long sidereal day give Venus a true daylength (from sunrise to sunrise) of 177 Earth days.

Venus' slow rotation explains another difference from Earth: this planet has a very weak **magnetic field**. On Earth the magnetic field comes from molten metal spinning in the planet's **core**. However, on Venus the rotation is so slow that the magnetic field is much weaker.

*This computer image, generated from data sent to Earth by the Magellan **space probe**, shows the tallest mountain on Venus: Maxwell Montes (centre, behind the mist). Maxwell Montes is about 11 kilometres (7 miles) tall. Mount Everest, Earth's tallest mountain, is only 9 kilometres (5.5 miles) tall.*

You might expect a planet with a four-month night to have a very cold dark side, but your spaceship's sensors indicate that Venus' night side is almost as scorching as its day side. This is because the planet's **atmosphere** acts like a thick blanket that keeps heat from escaping back into space. The odd difference in the lengths of the planet's year and day also means that Venus doesn't have seasons as we know them, so the climate is remarkably constant during the year.

The weather forecast for the surface of Venus never changes: hot, overcast and stormy, with sluggish winds. The Sun is just strong enough to shine dimly through the overcast sky. Despite the thick clouds, it never rains on the surface of Venus. A sort of rainfall occurs at the bottom of the cloud layer, where droplets of concentrated **sulphuric acid** fall out of the clouds. However, the searing heat makes the droplets evaporate long before they reach the ground. Thunderous lightning bolts tear through the sky over the volcanoes, sometimes at rates of 25 bolts per second. The winds pick up at the base of the cloud layer, and blow from east to west at about 150 kilometres per hour (90 miles per hour).

*This series of photographs taken by a Pioneer **space probe** in 1979 shows how quickly the cloud patterns on Venus change. The dark V-shape in the centre is formed by high winds that sweep from the equator to the poles.*

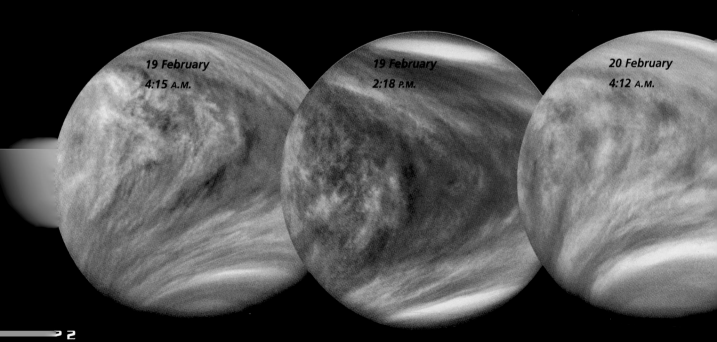

19 February 4:15 A.M.

19 February 2:18 P.M.

20 February 4:12 A.M.

Venus' high winds are driven by hot air over the **equator** spreading to the planet's **poles**, where the temperature is cooler. The winds get faster higher up in the atmosphere, reaching a maximum speed of about 360 kilometres per hour (225 miles per hour) at the cloud tops.

The clouds are yellow because they contain **sulphur compounds**, such as sulphur dioxide and hydrogen sulphide. A dark V-shape, visible from space, is the result of changing concentrations of sulphur compounds as the clouds are swept by high winds. Venus' cloud pattern is fairly simple because the planet spins slowly, causing the wind to spiral around the planet as it moves from the equator to the poles. In contrast, Earth has complex cloud patterns because it spins much more quickly.

RIGHT: *Dramatic bolts of lightning, like this one photographed over the mountain backdrop of Tucson, Arizona, can also be seen over volcanoes on Venus.*

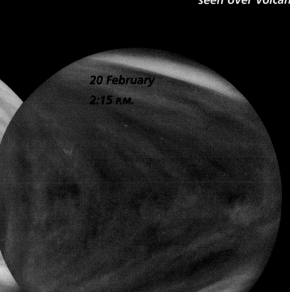

20 February
2:15 P.M.

How did Venus get so hot?

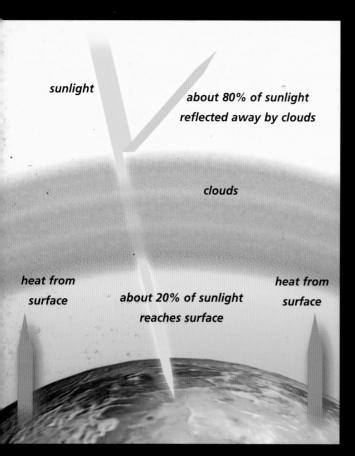

sunlight

about 80% of sunlight
reflected away by clouds

clouds

heat from
surface

about 20% of sunlight
reaches surface

heat from
surface

This diagram shows Venus' greenhouse effect. Sunlight warms the ground, then heat released is trapped by carbon dioxide in the dense atmosphere.

From the safety of your spaceship in **orbit**, you reflect on the strange planet you've just visited. What made it so different from Earth? According to astronomers, it all comes down to one thing: Earth has huge amounts of water in its oceans and **atmosphere**, but Venus has almost none.

Water is an important part of Earth's environment. If the Earth did not have so much water, there would be a much higher level of the gas **carbon dioxide** in our atmosphere. The water in clouds and rain reacts with carbon dioxide to form a weak acid, which then reacts to form minerals called carbonates when rain falls on rock. Carbonate minerals are very widespread on Earth and lock up huge amounts of carbon dioxide. On Venus there is no water, so all the carbon dioxide builds up in the atmosphere. This is why Venus' air is so **dense** and choking.

Carbon dioxide is a **greenhouse gas** – it lets sunlight reach a planet's surface, but it traps heat rays from the Sun-warmed ground. On Venus the greenhouse effect is so powerful that it keeps the surface temperature at about 475°C (900°F), which is hot enough to melt lead.

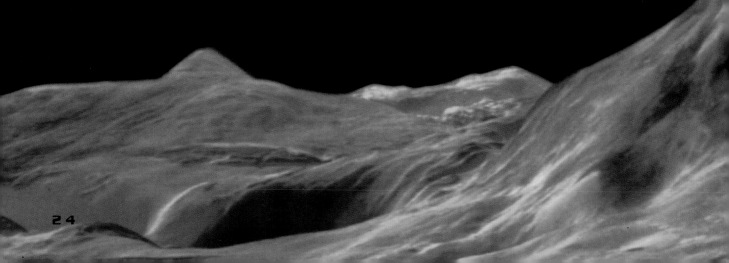

Did Venus have oceans?

*Venus is too hot for water to exist as a liquid today. Yet billions of years ago the Sun was dimmer and Venus was cooler. Perhaps it had oceans, as shown in this computer-generated image of Venus flooded with water. As the Sun got hotter the oceans would have evaporated. High in the atmosphere, the intense sunlight would have split water **molecules** into hydrogen and oxygen, then blown the hydrogen away into space, leaving the planet choked and dry. We may never know – any evidence of oceans would have disappeared under Venus' **lava** floods.*

Water, or the lack of it, may also explain why Venus has no **plates**. On Earth, water filters down into the hot **mantle** and turns into steam, which helps melt the rock and create a thin liquid layer called the **asthenosphere**. The asthenosphere is constantly moving, with the plates floating on top of it. On Venus there is no water, so there is no asthenosphere and no floating plates.

This photograph shows Venus' hot, dry landscape. It is kept this way by the carbon dioxide in the atmosphere, which traps heat at the planet's surface.

Myths and legends

Venus was known by the earliest astronomers, and it featured in many myths and legends. **Astrologers** also considered it an important and powerful planet. However, it was not until the invention of the telescope that people began to get an idea of what it was really like.

Because Venus is only seen just after sunset or just before sunrise, some early peoples thought that it was two different objects. The ancient Greeks knew better. They realized that Venus got closer and closer to the Sun in the morning sky before vanishing and then reappearing in the evening sky, but they still gave the planet two names: Phosphorus (the morning star) and Hesper (the evening star). It was the Romans who gave Venus the name that has stuck with it until today. Because of its brilliance they named the planet after their goddess of love and beauty.

The earliest recorded observations of Venus come from the civilization of Babylon, around 2000 BC. The Babylonians called the planet Ishtar, after their chief goddess, and made accurate records of its movements in the belief that doing so would help them to predict the future. Their records, carved in stone on the so-called Venus tablets, have helped today's historians pin down the dates of specific events in Babylon.

ABOVE: *This carving, made by one of the ancient civilizations in Guatemala in Central America, shows a human heart being offered as a sacrifice to Venus.*

BELOW: *The Mayans thought that the planet Venus could warn them of danger. To be able to closely observe its movements in the sky, they built this astronomical observatory at Chichen Itza in Mexico.*

Venus was the goddess of love and beauty in ancient Rome and later became a source of inspiration for many Italian Renaissance paintings, such as this one by Sandro Botticelli.

The Chinese also admired Venus, calling the planet Tai-pe, the beautiful white one, but the ancient Mayans of Mexico and Guatemala saw the planet as threatening. They built huge observatory temples to track Venus' movements, and worked out detailed calendars to predict when Venus would reappear in the morning sky before sunrise, an event they thought was especially dangerous.

In medieval Europe astronomy and astrology were closely united. Astrologers who studied the movements of Venus believed it controlled love and affairs of the heart. Astronomy only became a separate science in the 1500s. It was revolutionized around 1610 when Italian astronomer Galileo Galilei looked at the sky for the first time through a telescope and discovered the **phases** of Venus.

Because Venus showed a full cycle of phases, it meant that the planet must travel around the Sun. At the time, however, most people believed that the Earth was the centre of the Universe and that all the planets and stars went around it. Galileo's observation of Venus was one of the most important pieces of evidence in overthrowing this old way of seeing the Universe.

Venus before space probes

Before the invention of **space probes** astronomers had to work hard to learn anything about the conditions on Venus. Even as recently as the 1950s, our picture of Venus was incomplete and often wrong.

Galileo saw no markings on the surface of Venus but, as telescopes improved throughout the 1600s, several other astronomers thought they did. Many of these markings were just illusions, but this did not stop some astronomers from publishing maps of the surface. The Italian astronomer Gian Domenico Cassini, who made very accurate measurements of Mars's **rotation** from the changing marks on its surface, was just one of the victims. He claimed that Venus had markings that rotated in just over 23 hours.

In these early days Venus appeared to delight in playing tricks on astronomers. As well as seeing nonexistent marks on the planet, some astronomers claimed to have discovered a moon orbiting Venus. We now know that Venus definitely doesn't have a moon. The astronomers were probably just seeing double images of the planet reflected in their poor instruments.

In 1761 astronomers watched with interest as Venus passed across the Sun's face. Called a **transit**, this happens about twice a century and is due to occur next in 2004.

LEFT: *Venus shines brightly to the left of the Moon as dawn breaks over a lake on Earth.*

William Herschel
(1738-1822)

William Herschel, who was one of the first astronomers to see cloud patterns on Venus, is best known for discovering the planet Uranus. Born in Germany, Herschel moved to England to work as a musician, but he was fascinated by astronomy. The telescopes he built for himself were the best at the time, and the discovery of Uranus bought him so much fame that he became private astronomer to King George III.

During the 1761 transit the Russian astronomer M.V. Lomonosov noticed that the edge of Venus' silhouette appeared blurred. He guessed that the planet might be covered by a thick **atmosphere**. His theory was backed up by the two greatest astronomers of the late 1700s: Johann Schröter (discoverer of the **ashen light**) and William Herschel. Schröter and Herschel were probably the first people to see genuine cloud patterns on Venus, although Schröter also claimed he could see mountains sticking through the clouds.

In the 19th century astronomers and the general public became fascinated with the idea of life on Venus, and debate raged over whether the thick clouds hid lush jungles or a barren desert. Some people even suggested the ashen light was caused by forest fires or city lights.

By the early 20th century, improvements in telescopes and photography allowed the blurry clouds to be studied more closely, and before long the distinctive V-shaped cloud pattern was spotted. In the 1950s French astronomers studying the V-shape discovered that the upper clouds were circling Venus once every four days. Soon after that, scientists bounced **radar**, which consists of short pulses of radio waves, off Venus' surface. This allowed them to calculate Venus' rotation rate.

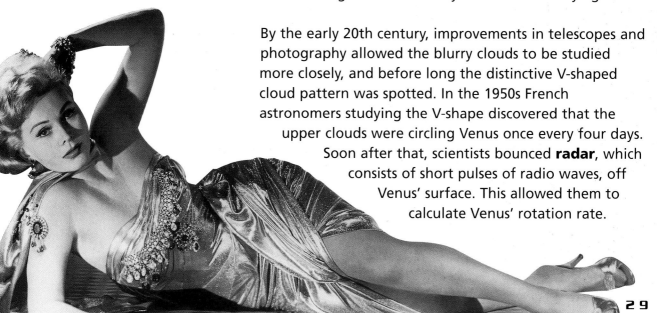

BELOW: *Actress Zsa Zsa Gabor plays a Venusian scientist in the 1958 film* Queen of Outer Space. *Before space probes proved otherwise, people thought Venus might be inhabited, and science fiction stories about life on the planet were popular. In* Queen of Outer Space *Venus was peopled only by women.*

Early probes

The first **space probes** to send back information about Venus were part of NASA's Mariner project. They were small, lightweight (only about 200 kilograms or 440 pounds), and were built in pairs so there was always a backup if something went wrong with the first one.

This was just as well, since *Mariner 1* had to be destroyed shortly after launch in July 1962 when a faulty rocket sent the probe hurtling towards a populated area. After corrections had been made, *Mariner 2* was launched a month later, and reached Venus safely in December 1962.

Because *Mariner 2* had to be kept lightweight, it could not carry the rockets and fuel necessary to slow it down and put it into **orbit** around Venus. So the probe just made a brief **flyby** before disappearing into space again. During the short visit the probe's sensors made some major discoveries. They revealed that the Venusian **atmosphere** is almost entirely **carbon dioxide**, they accurately measured the surface temperature for the first time, and they established that Venus has only a very weak **magnetic field**. *Mariner 5* returned to Venus in 1967 and confirmed the earlier findings, and *Mariner 10* flew past in 1974 on its way to Mercury, taking more than 4000 photographs of the Venusian cloud tops.

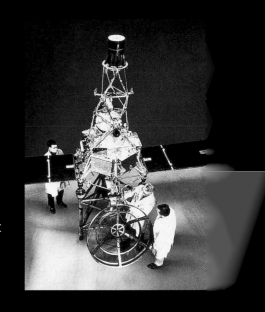

ABOVE: **Mariner 1,** *the first probe built to study Venus, was only 3 metres (10 feet) long and 1.5 metres (5 feet) wide.*

BELOW: *The Russian space probe* Venera 13 *took this amazing colour photograph of Venus' surface in 1982. The plates of rock probably formed in a* **lava** *flood. A camera cover (left), colour chart (right), and landing platform (centre bottom) can also be seen.*

The Soviet Union at this time, however, was more interested in what lay beneath the clouds. From 1961 onward they launched a series of Venera probes to land on the surface, though they didn't succeed in reaching Venus until *Venera 4* in 1967. This probe parachuted into the atmosphere but was destroyed by heat and pressure when it was still 25 kilometres (16 miles) above the surface. *Veneras 5* and *6* got a little closer, but still stopped transmitting at about 14 kilometres (9 miles) up.

In 1970 *Venera 7* made it to the surface. The engineers lost contact with the probe before touchdown, but reanalysed the data several weeks later and discovered a faint signal from the probe recording temperatures of 475°C (890°F) and an atmospheric pressure 90 times greater than that on Earth. Because the signals were constant, the engineers knew the probe had finally landed on the surface of Venus.

More **missions** followed. In 1975 the first pictures were sent back from the surface, and in 1982 *Veneras 13* and *14* carried chemical toolkits to analyse Venusian rocks.

ABOVE: Mariner 10 *took thousands of photographs of Venus' cloud tops as it flew past the planet on its journey to Mercury in 1974.*

Mapping from space

The Venusian **atmosphere** makes it hard for astronomers to get a clear view of the entire planet's surface. However, there is one technique that makes it possible to see through the clouds to the solid ground below: **radar**.

The principle of radar mapping is simple. A **space probe** fires a short pulse of radio waves at Venus and then measures the time it takes for the faint echo to bounce back. Radio waves can pass straight through clouds. Because they travel at a fixed speed, the time they take to return can be used to calculate the precise distance to the ground. Provided the probe is in a steady **orbit**, the distance to the ground can be converted into information about the ground's changing height.

The first detailed radar maps of Venus were made by NASA's *Pioneer Venus* space probe. This probe went into orbit around Venus in 1978 and continued to send back data until the 1990s. *Pioneer Venus*, along with two Venera probes in the 1980s, showed that most of Venus' surface is made of flat plains, with just a few raised areas and a scattering of tall mountains.

RIGHT: *A colour-coded radar map of Venus, produced by the Magellan probe, reveals the height of surface features. Highlands are pink and low ground is blue. If Venus had water, the blue areas would be oceans.*

BELOW: *The Magellan probe took about two years to map Venus. This artist's impression shows it beaming data back to Earth as it builds up a map of the surface (bright area).*

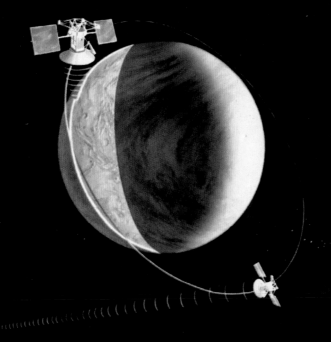

Pioneer Venus' radar was limited, so NASA launched the more sophisticated *Magellan* probe in 1989. It was named after the Portuguese sailor Ferdinand Magellan (1480–1521), the first person in history to lead a successful around-the-world expedition, though he himself died before finishing the journey. The *Magellan* probe carried an instrument called a synthetic aperture radar (SAR), which was used to make a highly detailed map of Venus' surface.

Magellan was a huge success. It surveyed 98 per cent of Venus' surface and mapped details that measured just a metre across. It revealed for the first time the full extent of Venus' volcanoes, craters and canyons.

After *Magellan* finished mapping Venus in 1992, its radar was turned off. Scientists then watched carefully as it continued in its orbit. By tracking wobbles in *Magellan*'s path, they were able to map changes in Venus' **gravity**, giving clues to the planet's interior. As a grand finale, *Magellan* plunged into Venus' atmosphere in October 1994 and burned up in a ball of fire.

Venus in 3-D

Many of the most spectacular images of Venus' surface are generated by computers, using radar data sent to Earth from the Magellan *space probe. The computer produces a 3-D rendering of the surface to show canyons, hills and other raised features. This image shows a deep canyon cutting through part of Venus' highlands. As in many such images, the heights of all features have been exaggerated. In reality Venus is much flatter than it appears here.*

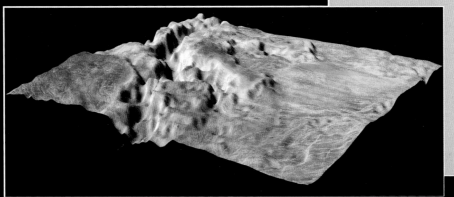

Lessons from Venus

In recent decades scientists have learned a great deal about Venus, and we now have a clear idea why the planet is so different from Earth. But Venus is also a warning of what Earth could one day become.

Earth has a comfortable climate because most of our planet's **carbon dioxide** is locked up in the ground. Carbon dioxide in the **atmosphere** dissolves in rain, and then combines with rock when the rain falls on the ground. But many people are worried that pollution is increasing the level of carbon dioxide in the air and giving our planet its own greenhouse effect, though on a much smaller scale than on Venus.

In the distant future, Earth could become a roasting, waterless desert, just like Venus (artist's impression).

Venus could also be a vision of our planet billions of years in the future. As the Sun gets older it will slowly get hotter, and eventually it could warm the Earth so much that the oceans evaporate. With no more rain to remove carbon dioxide from the air, a runaway greenhouse effect could set in. Ultimately, the Earth's **plates** might even grind to a halt, and our planet would turn into a true twin of Venus.

Could humans live there?

Today Venus is the most deadly planet in the Solar System. Other planets might be too hot or too cold, but none would kill you so quickly, and in so many ways, as Venus.

Billions of years ago, though, things might have been very different. According to some experts, Venus once had enough water to cover its surface to a depth of 9 metres (30 feet). The oceans were probably warmer than Earth's but, even so, simple forms of life might have found a foothold there.

Venus' volcanoes could have helped life to get started. In 1977 scientists on Earth discovered that hot springs in the ocean depths, called black smokers, are havens for unusual forms of life. The smokers pour huge amounts of minerals into the sea around them, and giant worms and blind crabs are just some of the animals found there. Some biologists think that life on Earth might have begun around underwater springs like these billions of years ago, and something similar might have happened on Venus. Perhaps, deep beneath the recent **lava** floods, **fossilized** creatures lie waiting to be discovered.

*It is very unlikely that humans will ever visit Venus, let alone set up a base there. Only **space probes** can reach the surface, and even they are soon destroyed by the crushing atmosphere.*

Greening Venus

Although Venus is an inhospitable world, some people have imagined how it might be transformed into a second Earth in the distant future. This process, called terraforming, was first proposed in 1961 by Carl Sagan, a famous NASA astronomer and author.

Sagan's idea was to take advantage of photosynthesis, the natural process that plants use to make food, turning **carbon dioxide** into oxygen in the process. He thought that one day spacecraft might seed the Venusian **atmosphere** with simple plants, such as algae. Over thousands of years, these algae would absorb carbon dioxide and release oxygen, gradually reducing the greenhouse effect until the temperature was low enough for people to live on the surface.

Today we know what Sagan did not: that Venus has virtually no water vapour in its atmosphere. For his idea to work, water would have to be added from somewhere else, perhaps by diverting **comets** towards Venus, for instance. Comet impacts might also help blow away some of the gas in the atmosphere and make it less stifling. Another way of speeding up the process would be to place gigantic sunshields around Venus to block out the sunlight, but such a tremendous feat of engineering is beyond the capabilities of modern technology.

Carl Sagan (1934–1996)

Carl Sagan (right) – shown here with his wife Ann (left) – was one of the world's best-known astronomers, thanks largely to his TV series Cosmos *and his novel* Contact*, which was later turned into a film. As well as writing and broadcasting, Sagan was a serious astronomer, with a special interest in the search for* **extraterrestrial intelligence** *and the conditions required for life to begin on other planets.*

Glossary

artificial gravity force generated by a spaceship that enables astronauts to stand on the floor instead of floating in midair

ashen light strange pale glow in the atmosphere on the night side of Venus

asthenosphere layer of fluid, shifting rock below the Earth's crust. The plates that make up the crust float on the asthenosphere.

astrologer someone who practises an ancient tradition that people and events are influenced by the positions of planets, moons and stars

atmosphere layer of gas trapped by gravity around the surface of a planet

axis imaginary line through the middle of a planet or moon that it spins around

carbon dioxide heavy, colourless gas that dissolves in water. Carbon dioxide is found in the atmospheres of Earth, Venus and Mars.

comet large chunk of ice left over from when the planets formed. Comets grow long, glowing tails when near the Sun.

convection process in which hot materials rise and cold ones sink down to replace them

core centre of a planet or moon

crescent curved shape like one segment of an orange

crust solid outer surface of a planet or moon

debris fragments of rock, dust, ice or other materials floating in space

dense having a lot of weight squeezed into a small space

dormant asleep or no longer active, but might become active again

element chemical that cannot be split into other chemicals

equator imaginary line around the centre of a planet, moon or star that is located midway between the poles

extraterrestrial intelligence theory of intelligent life on other planets

flyby space mission in which a craft is going too fast to fall into orbit around a planet or moon, but collects information as it passes

fossilized preserved in rock within the planet's crust

gravity force that pulls objects together. The heavier or closer an object is, the stronger its gravity, or pull.

greenhouse gas gas in a planet's atmosphere that traps heat from the ground

igneous name used to describe rock that forms when magma or lava solidifies

impact crater circular crater made when a comet, asteroid or meteorite smashes into a planet or moon

lava molten rock that pours out of a volcano

magma molten rock beneath Earth's surface

magnetic field region around a planet, moon or star where a compass can detect the north pole

mantle part of a planet or moon located between the core and the crust

meteor small piece of space rock that burns up in a planet's atmosphere, producing a streak of light called a shooting star

meteorite space rock that lands on the surface of a planet or moon

mission expedition to visit or observe a specific target in space, such as a planet, moon, star or comet

molecule tiny unit of matter consisting of two or more atoms joined together

orbit path an object takes around another when it is trapped by the larger object's gravity; or, to take such a path

phase the amount of the sunlit side of a planet or moon that an observer can see

planetesimal small, planetlike ball of debris that formed in the early Solar System

plate part of Earth's crust that floats on the asthenosphere and collides with other plates

pole point on the surface of a planet, moon or star that coincides with the top or bottom end of its axis

radar technology using short pulses of radio waves to calculate an object's position or shape

rotation movement of a planet, moon or star turning around its centre, or axis

shield volcano type of volcano consisting of a huge cone of solidified lava with a circular crater at the top

sidereal day time taken for a planet to make one complete rotation

space probe robotic vehicle sent from Earth to study the Solar System

sulphur compound chemical consisting of a combination of sulphur and other elements

sulphuric acid powerful acid made from sulphur. It is found in Venus' clouds.

transit movement of a planet directly in front of the Sun, as seen from Earth

ultraviolet light type of invisible light given off by objects hotter or with more energy than objects that glow with blue or violet light

Books and websites

Couper, Heather, and Henbest, Nigel. *The DK Space Encyclopedia*. London: Dorling Kindersley, 1999.
Furniss, Tim. *The Solar System – Spinning Through Space*. London: Hodder Wayland (Hodder & Stoughton Children's Division), 1999.
Kerrod, Robin. *Our Solar System – Near Planets*. London: Belitha Press Ltd, 2000.
pds.jpl.nasa.gov/planets/welcome/venus – Venus NASA
www.jpl.nasa.gov/magellan – NASA Magellan
www.windows.ucar.edu – Windows to the Universe